Bear's Beans

By **Gary Sheppard**

Illustrated by **Gisela Bohorquez**

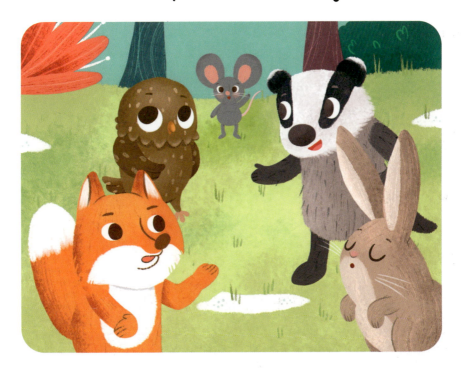

It was a sunny spring morning in the forest.

Owl, Badger, Rabbit, Fox and Mouse were happy

to see each other after the long, cold winter.

But someone was missing.

Bear's Beans

'Bear's Beans'
An original concept by Gary Sheppard
© Gary Sheppard

Illustrated by Gisela Bohorquez

Published by MAVERICK ARTS PUBLISHING LTD
Studio 11, City Business Centre, 6 Brighton Road,
Horsham, West Sussex, RH13 5BB
© Maverick Arts Publishing Limited November 2020
+44 (0)1403 256941

A CIP catalogue record for this book is available at the British Library.

ISBN 978-1-84886-713-0

www.maverickbooks.co.uk

Purple

This book is rated as: Purple Band (Guided Reading)

"Where's Bear?" Badger asked.

The others all shrugged. No one had seen him.

"He's probably still asleep!"

said Fox.

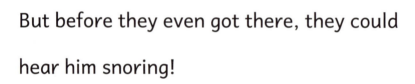

The friends headed up

the hill towards Bear's cave.

But before they even got there, they could

hear him snoring!

They found Bear fast asleep, curled up next to

lots of cans of his favourite food – beans!

He would eat them for breakfast, lunch and

dinner - even as a snack!

"How should we wake him?" asked Rabbit.

All the friends had different ideas

and each thought theirs was the best.

They soon started to argue.

"I can wake him," Mouse squeaked.

But no one could hear him over the noise.

"The problem is," boomed Badger, "Bear is just too warm and cosy. We need to make him cold! That will wake him up!"

Badger went outside. He returned a few minutes later with a barrow full of snow.

"Brrr! It really is cold!" Badger said. "If this doesn't wake him, nothing will! Okay everyone, pack the snow all around Bear."

So that's what they did.

The friends all stood and waited. But, although the cave was now much colder, Bear still didn't wake up. Soon the snow melted, and the friends continued to argue.

"I can wake him," Mouse squeaked. But once again, his friends couldn't hear him.

"The problem is," Owl hooted loudly, "it's too dark in here. I don't mind because I can see in the dark, but Bear doesn't know it's time to wake up."

Owl flew out of the cave. She returned a few minutes later, carrying some small mirrors.

"Okay everyone, grab a mirror and stand outside of the cave." So that's what they did.

The sun's rays bounced from mirror to mirror, and soon the dark cave was full of bright light. But Bear's eyes were still firmly shut.

Yet again, the friends all started to argue.

"I can wake him," Mouse said for the third time.

But once again, his friends were too busy arguing.

"The problem is," screeched Fox, "it's just too quiet in here! What we need to do is make as much noise as possible! That's sure to wake him up!"

Fox went outside. When she returned a few minutes later she was carrying lots of pots and pans. There were big ones, small ones, silver ones and coloured ones.

"Okay everyone, grab some pans and hit them together as loudly as you can!"

So that's what they did.

There was such a noise that it could be heard for miles around. CRASH, BANG, BASH! CRASH, BANG, BASH!

Surely Bear couldn't sleep through that? But he was still fast asleep. Once again, the friends started to argue.

This time, Mouse said nothing. But he knew _exactly_ how to wake Bear up.

Mouse walked out of the cave. A few minutes later he returned, carrying sticks he'd gathered from the forest floor.

"What are you doing, Mouse?!" Rabbit scoffed.

"A few old twigs won't wake Bear!"

But Mouse just ignored him and stacked

the sticks into a pile.

He then picked up one of the small pans that Fox

had brought.

"What are you doing, Mouse?" said Fox. "We've

already banged the pans. They didn't work!"

Once again, Mouse ignored his friend

and placed the pan on the sticks.

Next, he picked up one of the mirrors that Owl had brought.

"What are you doing, Mouse?!" Owl asked.

"We've already used the mirrors. They didn't work!"

But once more, Mouse ignored his friend.

He held the mirror to the sun and angled it towards the sticks. After a few minutes they started to smoke and then started to burn!

"What are you doing, Mouse?!" asked Badger. "Bear is already too warm and cosy, a fire won't help!"

Once again, Mouse ignored his friend and

grabbed a can of Bear's favourite beans.

He opened the can and emptied it into the pan.

"What are you doing, Mouse?!" Rabbit asked.

"It's no time for eating! We're trying to wake

Bear up!"

This time, Mouse did reply. "That's what

I'm doing," he said. "Wakey, wakey, Bear!"

Minutes later, a bubbling noise came from the pan. The smell of beans wafted its way to where Bear lay.

"Pah!" said Rabbit. "Nothing's happening. Bear's still fast asleep!"

But suddenly, Bear's nose began to twitch!
Then one eye opened wide... and then the
other! Finally, Bear's mouth slowly opened,
ready to shout...

"Beeeeeeaaaaaaannnsss!"

Bear was awake!

"My favourite!" he said. "You should have woken me sooner!"

The friends had stopped arguing.

They were all lost for words. Except Mouse.

"Come on," he squeaked happily. "Let's eat!"

This time, everyone listened and the friends all tucked into the tasty beans.

Quiz

1. What does Badger use to make Bear cold?

a) Water

b) Snow

c) Ice cream

2. What did Owl bring?

a) Torches

b) Pans

c) Mirrors

3. Who had the plan to make lots of noise?

a) Rabbit

b) Mouse

c) Fox

4. What did Mouse gather first?

a) Sticks

b) Beans

c) Pans

5. What woke Bear up?

a) Noise

b) A smell

c) Light

Turn over for answers

Book Bands for Guided Reading

The Institute of Education book banding system is a scale of colours that reflects the various levels of reading difficulty. The bands are assigned by taking into account the content, the language style, the layout and phonics. Word, phrase and sentence level work is also taken into consideration.

Maverick Early Readers are a bright, attractive range of books covering the pink to white bands. All of these books have been book banded for guided reading to the industry standard and edited by a leading educational consultant.

Pink

Red

Yellow

Blue

Green

Orange

Turquoise

Purple

Gold

White

To view the whole Maverick Readers scheme, visit our website at
www.maverickearlyreaders.com

Or scan the QR code above to view our scheme instantly!

Quiz Answers: 1b, 2c, 3c, 4a, 5b